THE ESSENCE OF CREATION AND DEVELOPER

FABRICATION OF UNBOWED DEVIL

SUMEET KUMAR

ISBN 979-888546472-7

Sumeet Kumar

Sumeet Kumar , A adult who experiences many phases of
love in his life , get broked many times , stands up every

time and keep moving to the next phases of the life.In reality he is a writter as well as singer (as a hobby).

Very exciting and interesting fact about him is that he is aauthor of New era i.e. he starts his journey of writing at the age when he was going to schools to get the study . His some famous works i.e. Maturity Of Love (Genre - Love),Privacy For Dream (Genre - Middle Class), Army Squad ofLove (Genre- The Seperation of Army Love), 5 Days of Love(Genre- Temporarily Love), Th e Endearment Of Love(Genre - Historical Era Of Love), Social Destruction Indo-Pak (Genre - The Story of The Love At The Time Of Division Of India And Pakistan), Middle Class Soul (Genre - The Dreams of Middle Class), The Accursed Kanatpur (Genre -The Horrific Story Of A Village), Wrong Number (Genre -The Suspenseful Physco Killer Story), The Secrecy OfDeadly Midnight (Genre - The Suspense About a Crime),Fragile Religious Of Death (Genre- The Death Of A TrustfulPerson), Nature Vs Science (Genre - The Future Battle Between Nature And Science In A Horrific Way), Generic Man (Genre - The Dream of I.I.T), The Unconsious 12 Hours(Genre - The Illusion At Stage Of Comma), The StrangeBurden (Genre - The Burden Of Love) , Her Existence (Genre- The Female Pain In The Society) , Jockstrap Prize (Genre -The True Story Of A National Athlete) , H Man [Hindi] (Genre - Superhero Tragic Story), H Man [English] (Genre - Superhero Tragic Story) , Maturity Of Love [Englsih] (Genre - Love) and many more are available on various geners on the offcial platform of **Amazon, Flipkart and Notionpress**. You can buy them from there.

Contents

PREFACE

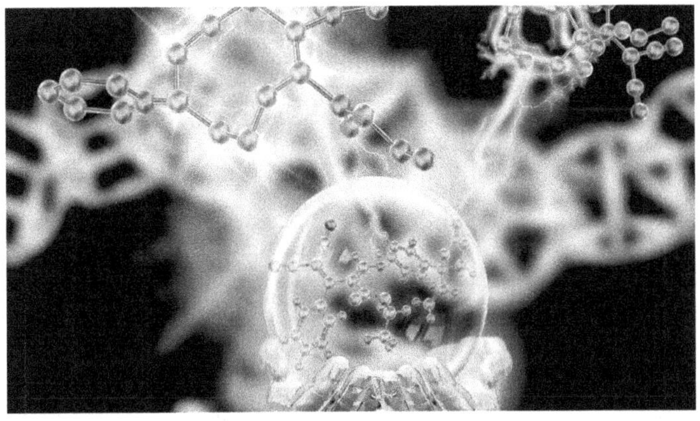

It is said that there is a big difference between Science and Emotions because Science gives us the thought to move forward, Vmotion forces us to move backwards undefined Garg: If I bring both of them together by mistake, I do not know that the world will remain, it is not undefined nor I I am science commanta, neither am anyone's emotions because if any one of me goes ahead, then it is harmful We can never change, we can try not to change. Today, even though with the help of science, all the big things that are not in the right of humans, I mean they cannot do the same work with the help of today's machines very comfortably. With its help, our country has increased so much, with its help, we have become more distant from ourselves. If you understand, it tests our love in such a way where defeat is sure. "Science does not matter in the field of love but love does not matter. In the field of science." I mean it is quite simple to say that we should never look at science and love from the same angle and never should I see it as one. I can't be one why I am saying this, what is the meaning of saying it will be known soon. If you are looking for something, then there is a science in it, even if death and life are also given to it. From the tears of the eyes to the pain of the heart, I have science in everything. In our society, there are two types. There is a log of those who do not believe in all this, their feet need to do it, a vlog who believes in science as everything. If it is not working, that is, there is unemployment, then there is science behind it because even though science has been made new by humans, but tomorrow it does not seem that science has been made by humans in truth. If seen, we are surrounded by science, the thought of this is present in this place. (Like if you want to ask your words to someone, we have to talk to someone, we do not need to be told, we sit on the cell phone while sitting at home. With the help of this you can ask the alphabet to anyone. If you want to see someone, you can do videocalls, all these are simple things, nowadays I am nothing more than this, there are such things which we never see, do not ever think about them .I had said earlier also that the thing which has its benefits, its disadvantages are more than that in the world. Just give it. Just like a plant is made from its seeds, just like science has become like a human being, so many feet are not able to tell how to tell. I appreciate everything in the world. From smile to big recognition. We live every day because our future is bad, no one ever thinks why we are like this today. Satkin' the Thinking off Our Future.

Acknowledgements

Aman Kumar

Special Thanks to **Aman Kumar** who worked so hard in the preparation of this book. He has continually put with my passive voice, omission of words, and late night calls. You have be en wonderful. Thanks to him for his precious time in reviewing proposals , individual chapters and early drafts, along with his suggestions on the applicability of the material to the world.

I
Virtual Science

Science, future, present, past are all the same, because it is a component as if a house is left behind like science is the parent of our future our past and still same for the present. Actually, it is the godfather of human now. All of you must be thinking that what is the relation of science and love since these two different sectors of our world. Up without science). There are many such morrs in life where we are compelled to think, after all, choose someone, because if you want love, science will have to be killed and if you want science, you will have to kill love, which is very difficult for anyone. I never said that science is behind someone's love. In our society, science has never been done against him, I will not say this like others Whose arrival has spoiled the relationship, we get away from you, because of this, the reason for spoiling the relationship is never science. Man is himself. Science is the only root. All are now dependent on science... actually the love and science in undefined we also look like same because undefined time the illusion is connected with them.and it beway like a human which had feelings of every human mentality.Mentality of science and mentality of a human is always same because when the Think for society it always remains same. But there was always a difference is under the science world is made up by human bangs and the human bangs is made up by the nature. I was not sure about under when the science was origin and where it Comes from because it always looks like a thinking of humans. The nature provides us many thing and they quick connect with the demand observe as thinking and the under observation moment is called science.(I mean to say that). If I can be honest then science was never born to us because it was earlier It exists from Yes.

"1. 5th century undefined 430bs- Empedocles provence under air is a material substance by sub merging ellipsis into the ocean.

2. 2nd Century: 240bs- Archimedes devises a principal which he later used to solve the riddle of the suspect crown.

3. 230 Bus- Arontosthenes Mysore the irthus circumference and dmtr.

4. 8th century ad- Jabir ibn Hayyan(Gabbar) introduced the experimental method and controlled experimental in chemistry.

5. 10th Century-Muhammad Ibn Zakariya Raazi(Rahas undefined introduced controlled experiment into the field of medicine and carried out the first medical experiment in order to undefined the mostigenic place to build a hospital."

Truth I speak toh it is nothing but all of human beings. Different from this thinking is that we always look at anything in one way only means that we always think about your benefit, try to move ahead with something or the other, feet never think that because of that We never think about the trouble we get. Nowadays, science is such a means that we do not believe in anything other than the thought of moving forward, and the more we are progressing with science, the more we harm the nature. Reaching us thinking we are killing him. Remain, when a destination starts moving, it should be left the same because it is not a means to move forward, I am such a fascination that no one can save from its havoc... Well this is just a story, my story is toh still left ....

"First of all, those who keep the Tishnagi of the Frog,
destroy your pond, if you have got the truth,
then I will become a city friend."

II
Left Science

Science is made by us we know under but your rights are
not made by us because your substance is love connected
with the nature world undefined I just want to say that
even though science has to stop every root of the foot

instead of the surgery things that helped us That it is nature's gift, we ask for the loss of both our past and present, in order to make a future. That everything is made of nothing. Due to which we have to face the shortage of oxygen and the trees which prevent those rivers from coming close, later due to their cutting, those rivers would take a huge form, due to which many houses, many localities, their yards, which they spent in their homes, leaving them behind. It's publicity. It's a very small reason why for everyone Because the house is lost, the life is not lost, when the birth will be done, what will be done after that, I am not saying that science is wrong, feet are any limit that in the world of everything, science also has a limit. It is the corona virus, which is becoming a myth nowadays, the reason for that is also a person's thinking somewhere, we always curse the upper one that why he does not listen to our batis so much he knows why. When God will come, why should we not be saved: the epidemic stops. Remember, nowadays science is wrong somewhere, so every human being is also wrong, why we are also associated with it, we have also harmed the present and the past. I am not saying that in today's society I should not move forward. Raise your leg as much as possible, as much as its limit If not the beginning, then the part of me that will come, he will have to suffer it. It is a question, not a profession, we start to move forward in our thinking, if we give the money used in thinking to a poor person, then his economic train is zero to number one foot toh toh aayegi foot nahi. If we look at his face, then we have to look at him so much that without looking back and forth, we go on covering his face in Maya. I don't know who has made us because till today I have never seen them, whoever made the feet, he made a human being, not even a single thought.

Why do we say that the present is also not right for us, if it is revealed, then there is some log, those who want to fix it, they can also deviate from your path. That much science has done experiments. If you have to experiment, then do it on the earth website instead of which nowadays Nothing is right, why do I need to say this that it will be known soon. That's why we have to give a limit to our thinking, why every time it is not true that our thinking should only walk with our feet because when this thinking progresses for some wrongdoing, then we think that we get a pond, which is not right for today's day. .If I take one wrong work of Vigan in front of you, then thousands of questions will arise from behind that science is not wrong, your thinking is wrong and many feet I am also saying here that science was never wrong, it is not wrong, so we have thinking and need to move forward. The way is the past, the way it is wrong. And there is some experiment which is wrong like we used to do different experiments on animals in order to move a person forward. Isn't it possible that they don't have the courage to live and we can raise our voices, but they are not, I can't give any knowledge I am not giving, I am a saint. Bash want to say that just as the above-mentioned animals have done the same thing. Nowadays there is no epidemic, so the reason for that is also we, because we have done the same thing because of the destruction of the world. Human beings always realize by doing wrong deeds, for this they will not get reprimanded, all have forgotten their karma. The word of name is also present in the world. Log knows that we cannot change the nature of nature, yet we try to change its texture, due to which our human race has also faced their troubles and disasters. There is a whiff of change, nowadays, how many logs are committing suicide due to social media because they are always afraid that after all, because of this. Let there not be mischief which becomes the cause of our death, if for the rest of our life we will share our thinking in the path of science, then the day is not far away when the world will be made of nafs but nothing else. Because in the world, every human being has to move forward six times, if not to change my thinking, then this way is not going to work for anyone, why am I wrong too? How can I be happy I don't know nor am I ever going to do this.....well Jishmanzil urges me to express my words to someone who walks on me undefined

""Today there is a pond in the shape of a pond,
everyone and
in the hope of the uncountable thinking that
we are moving forward,
the destination of it is also deserted, not
everyone knows................
By coincidence in her and ourselves,
we have made the desire to become God in our
wish. ....""

III
The Need To Think

1998 Vizag 24 Country This is such a story that changed the shadow of science, we can never make or change our destiny because it is the gift of the above, in whose glory everyone has feet nowadays. There are logs who try to change the texture of nature and its handwriting.

Whatever I am going to say today, it has happened like an accident and an accident. Every time, only someone's help has handled the other in every pain, in everyone's sorrow, he has shown the love of the family even though he is not a family. Dr. Ramanujan and his wife are Dr. Naira, residents of Toh V, Andhra Pradesh, India, although Ramanujan was an expert by profession, I mean a biotech scientist and his wife was a Mabbs qualified doctor. Everything is fine in their life because the happiness of a family is right for their children is undefined and the reason for the happiness of Ramanujan and Naira was a daughter whose name was very happy and with a lot of enthusiasm, they used to help each other, where the daughters used to enjoy the first meal. For V Ramanujan, his daughter was eccentrically everything, although he used to belong before a typical middle class. Her daughter was known by the name undefined, her daughter was so sweet that the society in which she lived did not talk about any other child except her. Like normal, it was not enough, it was normal, in which age children pay attention to play and there is not that much society in young age. was sharp Helping Nature Loviveribodya and much more The teachers who used to come to teach her did not have as many questions as Akantara had 36 answers for each question. By the way, Ekantara was born in 1990 when her parents had completed 8 years of marriage. Ramanujan, being a great scientist, had done many such experiments for Vizag, the government had done him several times with different awards for this. He used to observe as if he had given a new life to science. To be fair, no one could do his thinking in a sensual manner. It was also true. Their family is more popularly known as Tamil family and a super genetic family. It was known that before this such thinking had never been seen in any of his births, say that it was the family of Vaormanujan, it was from the family of Naira. To be silent, it was to be a child. All three of them were very happy among themselves. Without wealth, you can never think without orijat. We should always have such a thought, due to which everyone gets happiness, benefits of every karishi and that should be a new life for everyone.

""The thesis of everything given time to time but when it comes to someone great thinking its never DIE............""

ishi Everything in the world is made of science without science That is, if the foot is not tolerated by mistake, then the coming luck also changes your path due to its absence. Many times it seems that we can balance our life, feet are nothing like this, the balance of our life is also connected with our nature somewhere, if its composition changes, then every part of us says that it is happiness, it is sorrow, it is something. Even if it is not, no one can change it. Even though the distance of our thinking is in our hands, the luck of moving forward is not in our hands at all. Our thinking and luck also have a different way because these don cannot live without each other. Because where the thought has been born, the handwriting of luck is always there. Since the truth of this is incomplete till now the beginning has not flowed, so let's see what all Batati has to take from Ramanujan's family.

""Weirdest thing is mine, whose desire also passes through my path.........

*.......And how much helplessness should I pin up
inside myself
because now even its fate is waiting for my
veins."*”

• 11 •

IV
The Happiness in Life

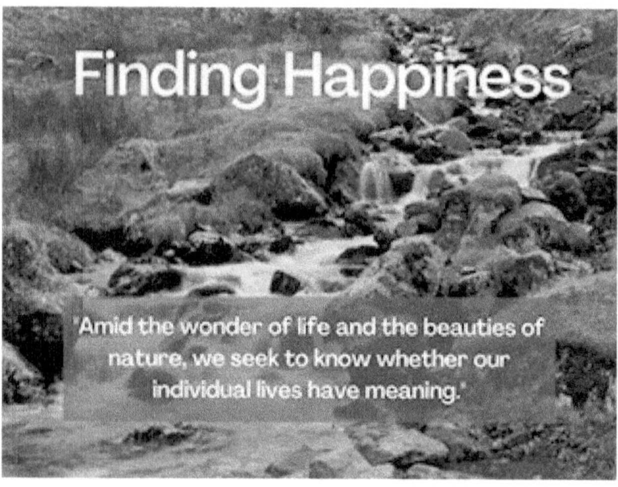

There also comes a time in which we lose everything, our happiness, our existence, our pond, our wish, too much, even by expressing which does not change anyone's condition, super genetic family, I am also going well. Everywhere there was happiness. Everywhere there was a different shadow. I was very happy with all these three feet · 17 · It is said that I do not get success as soon as I fail in the world, I mean there is no moment of happiness, it is always a shadow There is as much negativity as there is positivity because the balance of the don is equal in the world, if any one mistake increases, then the balance becomes very bad, the pond that is there also gets destroyed somewhere and those who try to get it Keep that cipher becomes a part of their existence only after becoming a jealous. I am saying that all the time, where the shadow of happiness kept the shadow of happiness, now he was about to break the watch of troubles and the person who has not considered his life as a problem. Had it been said by his family that he was the one who lost in front of anyone for the first time. If love is dear to us and it goes away from us, then it takes some time to erase its pain, my feet become weak, but when that pain is in someone's part, then that pain stays with us throughout life, it is a strange coincidence that in time you Even if something is worth the rule, that which is far away is in the hands of the cipher and time only. Where the feet were creating happiness everywhere and becoming a means for everyone, what they could not find to eliminate their loneliness. What will happen next. You have to be happy with something and you wish to be true to me, Tofush Kashi Kouparwala makes your pond. Where surgery happiness he already had, another such happiness was coming, whose expectation was not allowing him to sleep, I mean After all, her wish was fulfilled, it was non-pergrant because she was a doctor, so no one is better than her. I can know its symptoms, they say that if a thing is done with a Manus, then it will eventually get fulfilled and the wish that everyone was doing in the supergenetic family i.e. a son kivo was going to be fulfilled soon. If life meets with all the misery, then we are the same foot, our destination is multiplied. She was a pregnant lady at that time, yet she never left the pond of work, she used to pay more attention to your work than your children. The coming child is to be separate from their existence, it is said that when it is time for pregnancy, whatever the child has seen with his eyes, that man will observe one thing every time, not mine, but this was not the value of his family and nowadays the world of Thyduniya I don't even believe it. Foot road is always right, it's not necessary, it's what we think. And if I get that truth, then what is the need of the above, and we are talking about the balance of the body, that is, what am I doing? Another small little child was about to come, then the enthusiasm will be there. And not only for them, but whoever is related to them, whatever the relationship is, they were also very happy, one more thing is to be understood that if the world is your enemy. If not, your luck is your biggest enemy at a time when we cannot see it because nowadays the voice of Tohapani Nafs is not heard at all, so it was a single enemy who was sitting inside himself with a coil. It is said that with the passage of time, the pond increases even more, it is obvious that the pond of genetic family had increased to a great extent and had increased to such an extent that it became difficult for Naira to leave the house. Not because of Ramanujan and Ekantara, Ramanujan never used to say that his little son had any problem even because of hockey and Ekantara also never wanted his beloved brother to come, I really care more about Naira than Ramanujan It was because

Ramanujan had to be told not to be told because of work, so many times he used to live alone with him. Ramanujan took away every single thing from you who was trying to put an archan in passing time with his son and his family I mean trying to put stoppage on Khusiano. And when a month has passed and now It was time that the little life has now come to the world. It was then that life left the bright side and took the hand of the dark side, I had already said that life has many characters and many sides. For himself, his existence will become a disaster for his son, and he will be the reason for his death.
Yega undefined Toh Raho, why should we wait when Musafir is our own, because even if the destination is deserted feet, we know its paths, we are enough.....
"I am not dead under time when my soul is far from
ME... ....
I'm dead under time when the humanity of God is lost in the way of my family happiness......."

Really I don't die when every one of his ponds, every wish from him go to China a human being The time dies when someone snatches it from its existence is undefined and if your fate becomes the reason for your apprehension, then even revealing it does not get any kind of destiny, in fact, I know their little one for the super genetic family, everything for them Was.........

"The fate I have been wishing for all my life has turned out to be my destiny....
.With the power with which you have erased your grace,
May God make you aware of him.

then i will stop her feet before him showed her a glimpse..........""

V

The Intense Web Of Life

2000 24 Countries Super Genetic Family You never wanted to see the day in front of you, even though they were jealous of it while waiting for the day and the friends who made the day they never wanted in their life, the reason for the happiness of happiness was now Whey for them the cause of darkness was about to become what every cell was waiting for, that moment came with a new mask whose thought was hurting everyone at the same time the day Naira got labor pan then all the happiest time from the hospital Took it because the young woman had become a little quirky in pregnancy, due to which she was admitted to the board, she would have run the operation for more than the calculation of the work and the condition of Ramanujan who was lucky, no one guessed that it was a different China on the face. At the time of losing something, he was so scared that it was clear from his emotions that how much pain he was in, he used to say not to express his feet, because it was the same foot, the emotions are also amazing, but sometimes it feels like There is no control like this in reality, I can say that it is naturally infected. Whatever happens next to me, sometimes my feet feel irritable, it is such a guest, on whose arrival we get happiness and sorrow because sometimes it expresses someone's silence and sometimes it is someone's happiness. Let's see what is happening with Naira now, what is the condition of this super genetic family now. Without revealing the time, I am advancing the story for more than an hour, so listen carefully, the hours have passed and the doctors also win the bulbs. They were also able to come out one by one. Feet were not numb because of such a news that no one was present, who did not have the desire, which they could never even wish for. It was very difficult to walk, even if they wanted to, they could not do it, nobody knew; Science had done such a thing, which no one expected, Thai dinkhuda had such a ruckus that no one had any effort, you move the words forward, which is the way it is The name by which he was known to be recognized in the whole Sehar, that Pechan was about to be lost. Because that which was his wish, it became complete, with a different name of a different Hekafas, each of his boys was born on the same day. Is the world that exists, he did not have the same thing as Hayat's eyes, I mean he was blind from birth, he had eyes, feet, he was not a shish, he was not a vision, not a talisman by which he could see the existence of the world and which Somebody needs to worry about the streak, it was empty in his part, when everyone saw this, then all the people were in trouble, which I can not express in your alpha, nor can I be a part of their pain because neither I can feel that pain I can only come in his part, if even a little innocent God had shown a good time, no one would like pain and pestilence, when you are feeling so much pain in the words, then what must be happening with them, let us know first. Let's take it. The doctors from whom the young times had come, they called the first germs to you and He told everything and also said that he should deny Naira about it, why if she came to know about this, she would not be able to bear the pain, even when the loneliness was not so big, yet she was a different stage of society. He was disappointed when everyone was trying to hide each other's anger (I was frankly, what family was there, not everyone is happy to be together because anyone's company comes in front of a cowherd in the moment of pain undefined and the family That we are talking, she was already Gauhar, at that time Naira did not know anything because at that time she was not conscious nor did Ramanujan let her face what happened to her son. He was happy. Time was also with us, but time is also breaking, the legs were definitely broken and did not let Kishi break, even small children did not reveal that their family is in kissing time, the infidelity of the truth always hurts Naira. He did not get caught, but after a few days he came to know that the little son in whom he had never lost his eyes to his words. At his own time, he did not reveal what was the reason why he would not be able to see the brightness of his eyes. It happened that you punished us like this. He could not see anything instead of silence at the time, he knew that if we were having trouble because we gave birth to him, then how much trouble our son would be when he grew up and he would not be able to see the rosary whose Even today many Muslims lost their destination in Talaash, how will they see themselves, how they went to digest us, how will they see the world Ramanujan at the time Naira bash was asking this question and nothing. At the time, if the person felt the pain in which Naira is in pain, then she would not be able to handle herself, neither Naira nor her entire family. Nahi jino dunga I will make her better than this, she won't be able to stay in Naira. I will fix you sons above, we do not need any son, I will take someone forward, shut up, I will make everything right. He makes a mistake that in solving a question, we never pay attention to the solution of the second question, why am I saying Ash, I have to ask, I will show that the foot is still fine....

**"*Nor are those spectacles in my existence,*
whose death God has done without a
light........."**

VI

The Final Battle

One day after Ramanujan's saying that everything will be fine, I will take forward your son, there will be no problem, he will never become a helper to anyone in the world, he will not have any problem going ahead, after a few years when Akshu who was Ramanujan's son The name of Akshu was a year old with Purre, today not so much society, feet can feel the pain that they are healthy by looking at other children every day, they are not like them, feet are different, they forget to tell one thing to all of you I have lost even though the pond of seeing the world was only with those eyes which never saw the darkness and even though he had no lines in his hands, his feet were different. What will he do, he also got up on Helen Keller, who was both deaf and blind, no one could do what she did, even those who have both eyes and ears, still they say no when God is worried about something with graceful hands. So in return, he also gives a new pond, this is the time to move forward that his house, I mean super and genetic family Every human was a genius, feet more than those who used to see the truth with closed eyes, he could see it was quite different, just like Einstein. Started, he did research on his son's death for seven consecutive years. And in those seven years he never failed, he never gave up, because he himself can break the promise he made to the world. He could never tow her, why he was the only one whose path he could never leave. Because he was the best in everything, like all the logs in his family, he was also the most genius of them all, so no one ever dared to make fun of anyone questioning his shyness that he had eyes but he could see He could not, even if the lines of his hands were not, nor wherever his thinking used to step, it was his admiration. She also used to be silent, she felt that she had no emotion other than happiness, why she had never hurt anyone's lamps, even though Himatra was only a twelve-year-old left, in front of his spout and intelligent, scientists like Einstein and Nevton like hooks. Even though he was aware from the point of view of his feet, the things he felt by touching it was not a matter of anyone's bash, in those twelve years he had done so much, compared to which the common child is very far from him. It was only then that he cleared his 12th standard and started teaching microbilay, which till date no one has ever allowed himself to feel that he cannot see with his eyes. He always used to say that " Taray toh bekum perfect is better then employment .." And why should there not be such thinking why his family has not thought of any Nehru till today, so how could he have taken Nayat himself to China with the help of his eyes and the lines of his hands. He had accepted you as a means to move forward, he never wanted to give up. The feet say God You are the most capable man, you keep your feet connected, whatever trouble is in the hands of God, he gives most like a holy pond, not that he is committing a crime by giving all this to him, he is causing havoc, he has a reason to destroy him There is no such thing out of it, he knows that the pain which he is giving to the sage who is giving his rule in those hands, he will surely come out of it and not apologise, because even the smallest glimpse can be seen, then he Roshni becomes very depressed. Like her entire family was a pharaozan for her, her face was the only way to move forward for Akshu. The feet were told that you yourself only try the most capable person, most of the time, Akshu Even after a year, Ramanujan finally got such a meeting so that he could bring light again in the life of his son, his eyes which had a pond to see everything. That he could fulfill his wish, because Ramanujan had already done experiments on animals, due to which his eyesight came. Foot Ramanujan didn't know at all what the letter would do on the thing he had made. He never checked Akashu's eyes when his eyes were bad since childhood, even though he was born from the hollow of Naira, his DNA is not that at all Teh because there is a reason behind this which you all do not know, this is also what was used on Naira in the past, because of which the eyeshadow was not matching with them, there are some such secrets of science which till date no one has been able to find them. This was also a mystery out of which the Himmunodosi that Ramanujan had left to cure your son's disease, that cipher could be used only on human feet and not on the DNA of animals and the animal on which he had used this earlier was only a few days later. After Ramanujan left, he did not know that the murder was to be paid because the men did it: the specialty was that he worked at a very fast speed and it was necessary to give 48 horse-hour observation to whatever leg was used. Why did Ramanujan take the wrong decision why team observation time in Kaitualaya? Work was 72 horses feet. When he became Immundoz, he used his son's foot in 48 hours. Tha he completely destroys the DNA of an animal within 72 hours, his defeat kills a cell, foot he did not know this when he used ushimmunodosi on Akshu, before that he was scared of voicoffee, because of which he got this Had forgotten that it was necessary to have a match, that it was a human's leg only for that time it seemed that the DNA in the eye is that of human being, the leg was not of any human and the moment he gave his friend to the eye, his legs were completely The body had disguised as Half Wolf and Half Lion, that is, it used DNA from them. Was it made from the DNA of Half-Wolf and Half-Lion? In the body, they came to the dunkache of animals and what was the matter like this, because of which in 72 hours. Nor can he kill any animal Kelko and what happened after that when he got Immunodosi and came in the guise of half wolf and half lion, what other then purebred seher and Thai coming from super genetic family? ????

""I wish there was love with protection. (2)
And the grace I was looking for, finally gaves a word.............
JIN's eyes I wanted to have Farozan, she has become the reason for someone else's existence.........
It is not known when smile wins it took the path of the cipher.""

.... COMING SOON EDITION 2.........